*The Truth About Santa Claus*

# *The Truth About*

# Santa Claus

## *JAMES CROSS GIBLIN*

ILLUSTRATED WITH PHOTOGRAPHS AND PRINTS

HarperCollins*Publishers*

FRONTISPIECE: *Photo by R. G. Hennis, Vincennes, Indiana, 1925.*
THE LIBRARY OF CONGRESS.

The Truth About Santa Claus
Copyright © 1985 by James Cross Giblin
Printed in the U.S.A. All rights reserved.
For information address HarperCollins Children's Books,
a division of HarperCollins Publishers,
10 East 53rd Street, New York, NY 10022.
Designed by Trish Parcell
10   9   8   7   6   5

Library of Congress Cataloging-in-Publication Data
Giblin, James.
    The truth about Santa Claus.

    Summary: Explains how historical facts, religious
mythology, folklore, tradition, and commercial promotion
have combined to give us the modern figure of Santa Claus.
    1. Santa Claus—Juvenile literature.   [1. Santa
Claus]   I. Title.
GT4992.G52  1985        394.2′68282        85-47541
ISBN 0-690-04483-6
ISBN 0-690-04484-4 (lib. bdg.)

# ACKNOWLEDGMENTS

*For their help in providing research material and illustrations, the author thanks the following individuals and institutions:*

*Marcia Biederman*
*The Cleveland Museum of Art*
*Judy Cohn, Macy's, New York*
*Frieda Foertsch, Santa Claus Chamber of Commerce, Santa Claus, Indiana*
*Paul Galdone*
*Norma Goldsmith, Volunteers of America*
*The Library of Congress*
*The Metropolitan Museum of Art, New York*
*Montgomery Ward & Company*
*The New-York Historical Society*
*The New York Public Library, Central Children's Room*
*and the Mid-Manhattan Branch*
*Robert Quackenbush*
*The Rijksmuseum, Amsterdam*
*Dr. Agnes Stahlschmidt*
*Marvin Terban*
*Jane Zager, Burdine's, Miami, Florida*
*and*
*Norma Jean Sawicki*

ALSO BY JAMES CROSS GIBLIN

*Chimney Sweeps: Yesterday and Today*

*The Skyscraper Book*

*For Jeanne Prahl*

# Contents

*St. Nicholas. Oak sculpture, Flemish, circa 1500.*

# The Truth About Santa Claus

*Sidewalk Santas at breakfast before manning their collection posts on city streets.*

# CHAPTER ONE

# Who Is Santa Claus?

W ho is Santa Claus? Is he the jolly man sitting on a throne in the toy section of a department store? Or the skinny fellow who stands on a street corner at Christmastime, ringing a bell and collecting money for charity? Is he your school principal, who dresses up in a Santa suit to hand out presents at a party? Or your father, who plays Santa at a family gathering?

The truth is all of these people and thousands more are Santa Claus today. But less than two hundred years ago there was no Santa Claus as we know him. No fat little man in a red suit and fur-trimmed cap rode across the sky on Christmas Eve in a sleigh full of gifts pulled by eight tiny reindeer.

That image of Santa Claus came later. There were other gift-bringers in olden times, though. Like Santa, they rewarded children who had been good throughout the year and punished those who had been bad. One of these gift-bringers was a selfish old woman. Another was a troll. Another was a witch. And still another was a man named Nicholas who later became a saint.

This book tells about these early gift-bringers, and shows how the real Nicholas was gradually transformed into the fairy-tale figure of Santa Claus. The story begins over 1500 years ago, when Nicholas was born in a small village on the shore of the Mediterranean Sea, in what is now Turkey.

# CHAPTER TWO

# Nicholas the Man

Little is known of Nicholas's life—so little, in fact, that in 1969 the Roman Catholic Church questioned whether he had ever really lived.

According to biographies of Nicholas, written long after his death, he was born in the village of Patara in Asia Minor about A.D. 280. His father and mother had been married for some years and had begun to fear they would never be blessed with a child. They were overjoyed with their first-born son and christened him Nicholas, which means "hero of the people" in Greek.

Although he was sometimes lonely, being an

only child, Nicholas enjoyed school and went faithfully to religious services. His parents didn't spoil him. Instead they taught him to be modest and think of others before himself. As one biographer wrote, the family was "not so rich as to be boastful, but they had enough to support themselves and still give to the poor."

Then, when Nicholas was twelve or thirteen, his happy, carefree life was shattered. A plague hit Patara and both of his parents were infected. Within a week they died, leaving Nicholas an orphan.

Nicholas wasn't content to sit back and live on his inheritance, though. He gave much of the money to charity and devoted himself even more seriously to his religious studies. At the age of nineteen he was ordained a priest in the Christian church and made a pilgrimage to the holy city of Jerusalem. Soon after his return he was named Bishop of Myra, a city near Patara. Nicholas was still so young that people called him the "Boy Bishop."

Despite his youth, Nicholas soon earned a reputation for kindliness and wisdom. His good works inspired more and more people in Myra to join the Christian church, and its activities flourished. Then, in the year 303, the Roman emperor Diocletian com-

*Nicholas being consecrated Bishop of Myra. Stained-glass panel by Jacob Cornelisz, Netherlands, fifteenth century.*

manded all citizens of the Roman Empire, which included Asia Minor, to worship him as a god.

Christians believed in one god, and one god alone, so they could not in good conscience obey the Emperor's order. Angered by their stubbornness, Diocletian warned the Christians that they would be imprisoned and tortured unless they gave in. Still many resisted the Emperor's commands, including the Christians of Myra, led by steadfast Bishop Nicholas.

The Emperor carried through on his threats and imprisoned thousands of Christians, among them Nicholas. For over five years the Bishop was confined to a small cell. He suffered from cold, hunger, and thirst, but he never wavered in his beliefs. Whenever he had the opportunity, he urged his fellow Christians in prison to remain firm in their faith also.

At last Diocletian resigned and a more sympathetic emperor, Constantine, came to power. In 313 Nicholas was released from prison along with all other Christians who had been jailed because of their beliefs. Nicholas returned to his post as Bishop of Myra, and from then until the end of his life he worked hard to build up the church and convert more people to Christianity.

His years of suffering had made Nicholas even wiser and more understanding. By the time of his death on December 6, 343, people throughout Asia Minor had already begun to tell stories about his generosity and credit him with miracles. After he died these stories spread, and soon people started to call Nicholas a saint.

# CHAPTER THREE

# St. Nicholas

Shortly after Nicholas's death, a shrine was built at Myra to house his remains. People came from near and far to pray to him and ask for his support. By the year 450, churches in Asia Minor and Greece were being named in his honor, and by the year 800, Nicholas was officially recognized as a saint by the Eastern Catholic Church.

In the eyes of Catholics, a saint is someone who has lived such a holy life that, after dying and going to heaven, he or she is still able to help people on earth. When a saint is especially popular, he or she is often adopted by different groups of people as their patron saint, or special protector. This happened to

Nicholas. He became the patron saint of sailors, marriageable maidens, and children, and many legends sprang up to explain why he had been chosen by these groups.

In one of the best-known legends about Nicholas as the patron saint of sailors, a ship ran aground on sharp rocks during a severe storm off the coast of Asia Minor. As water poured through holes in the hull, the captain and crew thought the vessel would surely sink and they would all drown. In desperation they prayed to Bishop Nicholas. They had heard stories about his miraculous powers and hoped he might somehow be able to help them.

Suddenly the sailors looked up, and they gasped at what they saw. For there was Nicholas, clad in his red bishop's robes, flying down through the clouds toward them. As he landed on the deck of the ship, the winds ceased and the sea grew calm. The storm was over.

Nicholas joined the captain and crew in a prayer of thanks, then helped them to shove the ship off the dangerous rocks with long poles. At last the vessel was freed and, without another word, Nicholas flew up into the sky and disappeared as quickly as he had appeared.

*St. Nicholas stops the storm at sea. From THE BELLES HEURES OF JEAN, DUC OF BERRY.*

After the holes in the hull were patched, the ship sailed on to the port of Myra. There the captain and crew made a special pilgrimage to Nicholas's church. When they saw Bishop Nicholas again, standing beside the altar, they dropped to their knees before him. "How were you able to save us?" they asked.

Nicholas replied that, from an early age, he had been gifted with an ability to see people in danger, hear their cries for help, and go to their aid. He took no personal credit for this gift, saying that it was simply God's will. He urged the captain and all of the crew to devote their lives to God, too, and they promised that they would.

This story makes St. Nicholas sound like a distant ancestor of Superman, who could fly through the air when he spotted someone in trouble. It may also help to explain why the saint, after he became transformed into Santa Claus, was pictured as riding across the sky on Christmas Eve to deliver his gifts.

The legend that tells how Nicholas became the patron saint of marriageable maidens also portrays him for the first time as a gift-bringer. It happened when Nicholas was a well-to-do young man, before he became a bishop. One day he heard the sad story of a once-wealthy merchant in Myra who had lost all his money and was now deep in debt.

This man had three lovely daughters of marriageable age, but as he had no money for their dowries, no suitable young men wanted to marry them. Rather than see them—and himself—slowly starve, the man decided there was only one thing he could do: sell his first daughter into slavery.

After hearing the story, Nicholas wanted to do something to save the young woman from this terrible fate. But he knew that he could not approach the merchant directly. The man would be too proud to admit that he needed help. So, late one night, Nicholas filled a bag with gold, hurried through the dark streets to the merchant's house, and tossed the bag through an open window. Then, keeping to the shadows, he hurried back to his own home.

The next morning, the poor man found the bag of gold when he arose. At first he thought it must be false, but after rubbing the gold dust between his fingers, he realized it was genuine. He tried to imagine who had given the gold to him, but could not. At last he decided it must be a gift from God, and he proceeded to arrange a good marriage for the oldest of his three daughters.

*Nicholas providing dowries for the three poor maidens. Painting on wood by Bicci di Lorenzo (1373–1452).*

The merchant was sure he would never be in such a desperate state again, but soon he was just as poor as before. He decided that he would have to sell his second daughter.

Again Nicholas heard of the poor man's plight, and again he went to the man's house late at night with a bag of gold, which he tossed in through a window. The man found it in the morning, and arranged for the marriage of his second daughter.

The man was sure his troubles were over now, but soon he was as poor as ever. This time, though, instead of making plans to sell his third and last daughter, he waited at night in the shadows near an open window of his house. For he was certain his mysterious benefactor would come again, and he wanted to see who it was.

Sure enough, Nicholas arrived the next night and threw yet another bag of gold in through the window. As soon as the girls' father saw it, he ran outside and down the street and, in less than a minute, he caught up with Nicholas.

He recognized the young man at once, since Nicholas was already well known in Myra. Bowing down before Nicholas, he said, "Thank you, good sir, thank you. If the Lord in his compassion had not awakened your pity, then long before this my three daughters and I would have perished."

Embarrassed, Nicholas asked the man to rise and made him promise never to tell anyone who had helped him and his daughters. The man kept his word.

Only on his deathbed did he reveal that Nicholas had been the one who saved his family.

Once the story of Nicholas's good deed became known, it spread quickly throughout Asia Minor. After his death it was one of the legends that people cited to justify his being called a saint.

This legend also has connections with several Christmas traditions. In Sweden and other northern European countries, gift givers dressed as St. Nicholas sometimes throw gifts through an open door or window, and then dart away, just as Nicholas threw the bags of gold through the windows of the poor man's house.

And, in a different version of the legend, it is said that the three maidens, before going to bed, hung their freshly washed stockings near the fire to dry. According to this version, Nicholas tossed his bags of gold through a smoke hole in the wall. The bags landed in the girls' stockings, where they were discovered the next morning.

Children hearing this version of the tale may have been the first to hang their stockings by the fire. Like children today, they hoped that St. Nicholas would fill the stockings, not with bags of gold, but with small Christmas presents.

\*     \*     \*

The name day of a saint is the day on which he or she died. Soon after Nicholas's death, people started to celebrate his name day, December sixth, and new legends connected with that day began to circulate. One of them helps to explain why Nicholas became the patron saint of children.

In this story, a band of Arab pirates landed on the shore near Myra one December sixth and kidnapped a fisherman's son named Basil. They carried him back to their land and made him a cupbearer in the palace of their ruler.

A year later Basil's mother, still grieving, was reluctant to honor Nicholas on December sixth. Her husband persuaded her to do so, however. They went together to the church where Nicholas was buried and prayed for their lost son.

That evening the parents were just sitting down to eat in the courtyard of their home when the dogs began to bark. The father went to the gate, and when he opened it, he saw Basil standing there, dressed in Arab clothing and holding a silver cup.

The boy told his amazed parents that he had been helping to serve a meal on the terrace of the ruler's palace when he suddenly felt himself being raised up into the sky. He turned to see who was holding him and gazed into the kindly eyes of St. Nicholas. Nicholas called him by name, told him not to be afraid, and said he was taking Basil home because his parents had prayed so strongly for him that morning.

When Basil had finished, his parents hugged him, and then the three of them sat down to the happiest meal they had ever had. Afterward, they knelt in a prayer to St. Nicholas, who was responsible for their joy.

Legends such as this helped to establish Nicholas as the protector of children. They also convinced more and more people that he could perform miracles. Every year hundreds of the blind, deaf, and crippled made pilgrimages to Nicholas's grave in the hope that he would cure them of their ills.

When sailors from Italy stopped at Myra, they heard the stories about Nicholas and saw the lines of pilgrims at his tomb. Upon their return home, the sailors told their friends and neighbors about the saint and the amazing things he could do. The stories spread throughout Italy, and people began to wish that they could visit Nicholas's tomb themselves.

A band of merchant seamen from the Italian port city of Bari made this wish a reality. In the spring of

1087, after delivering a load of grain and other goods to Antioch, they sailed on to Myra and asked the way to Nicholas's shrine. Like many Italian Christians, the sailors were fearful that Nicholas's remains might be captured by Muslim raiders if they stayed in Myra. So they planned to seize the holy relics and bring them back to their home port of Bari where they would be safe.

Disguised as pilgrims, two of the fifty sailors went ahead to inspect Nicholas's shrine, which was located on a lonely headland. They reported back that it was guarded by only four custodians. The other sailors returned to the shrine with the two scouts, quickly overcame the guards, and broke through into Nicholas's tomb.

After wrapping his bones in a silken cloth, they hurried back to their ship, put Nicholas's remains aboard, and sailed away before their theft could be discovered by the citizens of Myra. A week or so later, on May 9, 1087, the ship arrived in Bari where the sailors were greeted with cheers and songs of praise.

A magnificent basilica, the Church of San Nicola, was built in Bari to house Nicholas's remains. Each year thousands of pilgrims visited the basilica, hoping, like the people of Asia Minor before them, that Nicholas would answer their prayers. Throughout Italy, Nicholas became a more popular name for baby boys than Peter or Paul.

Ships from all over Europe stopped at Bari, and soon word of Nicholas and his good deeds traveled to France, Germany, Holland, England, Sweden, and many other countries. Before long the tall, thin Bishop of Myra began to change into the gift-bringer we know today.

# CHAPTER FOUR

# St. Nicholas,

# the Gift-Bringer

Gift giving in the winter months had a long history in Europe before St. Nicholas became a gift-bringer, and even before Christmas began to be celebrated as the birthday of Jesus Christ in the fourth century A.D. The owners of large estates had often given gifts of fruits, nuts, and cakes to their servants and farm workers after the harvest was in. This led to much feasting and merrymaking around the Winter Solstice on December twenty-first, the longest night of the year.

St. Nicholas was by no means the first or only gift-bringer, either. In Spain, children believed that the Three Wise Men brought them gifts on January fifth. That was the eve of Epiphany. On Epiphany, January sixth, the Wise Men—three great kings from the East—were supposed to have visited baby Jesus in the stable at Bethlehem and given him gifts.

Other European gift-bringers also came on Epiphany Eve. Italian children were told that their gifts were delivered by the Befana, an old woman of Palestine who had been too busy with her housework to accompany the Three Wise Men to Bethlehem. The next day she regretted her decision, but it was too late to catch up with the Wise Men. Ever since, according to Italian legend, the Befana has traveled the world on Epiphany Eve, searching in vain for the Christ child. Along the way she leaves candy and other gifts in the shoes of sleeping children, hoping to make up for the gift she failed to give the Christ child.

Russian children were told a different version of this story. In it the Befana was Baboushka, a witchlike old woman who gave the Wise Men wrong directions when they asked her the way to Bethlehem. Like the Befana, Baboushka was condemned to wander the earth every Epiphany Eve. Quietly she entered house after house, peered at children in their beds, and placed gifts under their pillows. Perhaps one of the children was the Christ child, Baboushka thought, and he would forgive her for the mean trick she had played on the Wise Men.

Sweden was one of the few countries where the gift-bringer made his rounds on Christmas Eve, December twenty-fourth. He was the Jultomten, an elf who wore a red cap and had a long white beard. The Jultomten rode in a sleigh pulled by the Julbock, or Christmas goat, when he came to deliver his presents. Before going to bed on Christmas Eve, Swedish children often put out a plate of porridge for the Jultomten, along with some hay and carrots for his goat.

When people in the northern European countries—especially Holland, Germany, and France—heard about St. Nicholas, and the bags of gold he had given to the three poor maidens, they soon adopted him as their gift-bringer. The legend of the three maidens was adapted into a play. It was performed in churches on St. Nicholas's name day, and became an instant success.

In the small country of Holland, more than twenty-three churches were named for St. Nicholas by the end of the 1100s. Inspired by the saint's good deeds, worshippers in these churches started a new holiday custom. On December fifth, St. Nicholas Eve, they filled three wooden shoes with coins they had collected for the poor and put the shoes beside the front door of each church. The shoes symbolized the three bags of gold St. Nicholas had tossed through the window of the poor man's house.

The custom spread to other churches, and Dutch children took it up. They began to leave their empty wooden shoes by the fireside on St. Nicholas Eve, in the hope that the kindly saint would fill them with small gifts.

As Nicholas's popularity grew, people in Europe made up new stories about him that showed his concern for children. One of the most famous was first told in France about the year 1150. In it, three boys were on their way to enroll in a religious boarding school when they stopped at a country inn for the night.

The innkeeper saw that the boys were well-dressed and were carrying purses filled with money. Immediately he decided that the three would not leave his inn alive. He persuaded his reluctant wife to drug their food, and later, when the boys were sound asleep, he crept into their room and slit their throats. Then he and his wife cut up their bodies and put the pieces in a pickle barrel behind the inn where no one would ever think of looking for them.

The next day St. Nicholas arrived at the inn dressed as an old beggar. After asking the innkeeper for something to eat and being refused, Nicholas threw off his beggar's rags and revealed his bishop's robes underneath. He told the innkeeper and his wife that God knew of the terrible deed they had done, and they fell on their knees, begging forgiveness.

Nicholas invited the frightened man and woman to join him in a prayer. "We will ask God to bring the boys back to life," Nicholas said. "If He does, then we will know He has pardoned you. If not, you will stand condemned for all eternity."

Trembling, the innkeeper and his wife went outside and knelt in prayer with Nicholas beside the pickle barrel. After they had finished, they watched in stunned amazement as first one boy, then another, and then the third rose up out of the barrel. All three boys looked exactly the same as when they had arrived at the inn the day before.

"I slept very well," said the first boy.

"So did I," said the second.

*St. Nicholas bringing the three youths back to life while the inn-keeper and his wife kneel in prayer. Painting on wood by Bicci di Lorenzo.*

"I dreamed I was in Heaven," said the third.

St. Nicholas hugged each of the boys in turn, while the innkeeper and his wife wept tears of grat-itude because God had forgiven them.

Like the story of St. Nicholas and the three maidens, the story of the three students was made into a play and was performed in churches and schools all over Europe. The scene where the three boys rose up out of the pickle barrel always created a sensation. The play became a highlight of St. Nicholas Day celebrations on December sixth, and helped to establish Nicholas as the patron saint of students as well as children.

French schoolboys thought of other ways to honor Nicholas, both as patron saint and gift-bringer. In the 1200s, December sixth began to be celebrated as "Bishop Nicholas Day" in France. Several days beforehand, a boy from one of the religious schools in a French town or city was chosen to put on a bishop's red robes and tall headdress, and play St. Nicholas. He was called the "boy bishop" because Nicholas himself had been little more than a boy when he was elected Bishop of Myra.

December sixth was declared a school holiday. On that morning the boy bishop led a parade of his classmates through the streets of the town. As they marched, they sang songs in praise of Nicholas. Often they performed a play about him—usually the story of the three students—from a platform in the town square.

After the play, the boy bishop and his followers approached passersby and knocked on doors, asking for what was known as "bishop's money." Half of what the boys collected was spent on candles for the churches, the other half on candy and other presents for themselves.

Sometimes a special medal was made for the occasion. On it was engraved a likeness of St. Nicholas and the name of the boy who had played him that year. At the end of the parade, the medals were given to the boy bishop and all the other marchers.

By the 1400s, the custom of electing a boy bishop on December sixth had traveled from France to Germany, England, Holland, Belgium, and Switzerland. As the practice spread, the processions led by the boy bishop often became rowdy and violent. The boys roamed through the streets, playing pranks and sometimes beating up pedestrians. Instead of giving part of the money they collected to the church, they kept it all for themselves.

Many towns and cities reacted to such behavior by outlawing all St. Nicholas Day parades. In place of a boy bishop, a schoolmaster impersonated Nicholas at school celebrations and other gatherings on December sixth. Like a department store Santa Claus today, the teacher put on a red robe and long white beard, and interviewed the students one by one. He urged them to be good and then gave them small presents. These might be apples, bags of nuts, small cakes, or something useful like a quill pen.

Everyone didn't get a present. Boys who had been lazy or disobedient during the year received a small birch rod from the teacher instead. The rod was a warning to the boys that they would be whipped if they didn't mend their ways.

By the end of the 1400s, St. Nicholas was the third most beloved religious figure, after Jesus and his mother, Mary, in many European countries. Historians estimate that more than 2000 chapels, hospitals, and monasteries were named for him. On the eve of St. Nicholas Day, children in towns and cities all over Europe put out shoes and stockings for the saint to fill with presents.

Then, in the mid-1500s, the German religious leader Martin Luther led a movement to reform the practices of the Roman Catholic Church. One of Luther's main challenges was directed at the worship of saints, which he said was based largely on superstition. The celebration of St. Nicholas Day came under especially heavy fire from Luther. He denounced it as a holiday "in which so much childishness and falsehood are blended."

As Luther's Reformation movement spread across Europe, and the Protestant churches were established, more and more people questioned whether children should be taught to believe in St. Nicholas. Typical of the attacks on Nicholas was this verse by an unknown German poet of the late 1500s:

*The mothers all their children*
*    on the Eve [of St. Nicholas Day] do cause to fast,*
*And when they every one at night*
*    in senseless sleep are cast,*
*Both apples, nuts, and pears they bring,*
*    and other things beside,*
*As caps, and shoes, and petticoats,*
*    which secretly they hide,*
*And in the morning found, they say,*
*    that this St. Nicholas brought:*
*Thus tender minds to worship saints*
*    and wicked things are taught.*

Eventually, in most Protestant countries, the gift-giving celebration was moved from St. Nicholas Day to Christmas. At the same time, several new gift-bringers were invented to replace the old saint in children's imaginations. They came on Christmas Eve instead of December fifth. By the beginning of the 1600s, many European children grew up without ever hearing a word about St. Nicholas.

# CHAPTER FIVE

# Father Christmas, the Christkindl, and Sinter Claes

When people in England stopped worshipping St. Nicholas in the 1500s, they assigned his role as gift-bringer to the smiling figure of Father Christmas.

Actually, Father Christmas was an even older character than St. Nicholas. He grew out of the Roman god Saturn, who presided over the winter feast of Saturnalia. Roman soldiers brought the celebration of Saturnalia with them when they occupied England in A.D. 43, and after the Romans left the English adapted the holiday to their own purposes. Many of its traditions later became part of the English Christmas.

Father Christmas was usually portrayed as a gigantic man in a scarlet robe lined with fur. On his head he wore a crown of holly, ivy, or mistletoe. Like Saturn, he was a symbol of feasting, drinking, and other holiday merriment.

Father Christmas also served as a sort of master of ceremonies for the popular mummers' plays that were performed throughout England during the holiday season. At the beginning of the play, the actor performing Father Christmas strode onstage and recited this poem:

> *Here comes I, Father Christmas am I,*
> *Welcome—or welcome not;*
> *I hope old Father Christmas*
> *Will never be forgot. . . .*
> *Christmas comes but once a year,*
> *When it comes it brings good cheer;*
> *With a pocket full of money*
> *And a cellar full of beer,*
> *Roast beef, plum pudding, and mince pie,*
> *Who likes them better than I?*

While the English chose the nonreligious figure of Father Christmas to be their gift-bringer, the Germans went in the opposite direction. They told children that the Christ child himself—the *Christkindl* in

*The Christkindl. Drawing by Thomas Nast.*

German—was the one who brought them their presents on Christmas Eve.

German children put out bread baskets and plates for the Christkindl to fill with nuts, cookies, and candies. They believed that the holy infant traveled on the back of a pure white donkey, so they often left a small bundle of straw for the animal to eat. Of course the straw was always gone on Christmas morning.

The presents the Christkindl brought were called "Christ bundles." Besides food, the bundles contained caps, scarves, mittens, dolls, and small toys. Sometimes a birch rod, or "Christ rod," was tied to the bundle as a reminder to the child that he would be whipped if he wasn't good in the New Year.

In German Christmas celebrations, a small child— often a golden-haired girl—might dress up in a flowing white robe to impersonate the Christkindl. Angel wings were attached to the back of her costume, and on her head she wore a jeweled crown. Like the boy bishops in the old St. Nicholas Day celebrations, the Christkindl was the center of attention at German Christmas parties as she moved gracefully around the room, giving out gifts to the other children.

Only in Holland, among the Protestant countries, did people continue to worship St. Nicholas after Martin Luther's Reformation. This was partly because the Dutch were seafarers who still looked to Nicholas, the patron saint of sailors, for protection. Carved wooden likenesses of St. Nicholas appeared as figureheads on the bows of many Dutch ships.

According to Dutch tradition, the good saint returned to earth every St. Nicholas Eve. He wore his red bishop's robes and rode through the countryside on a magnificent horse.

Behind the saint, either riding on a mule or walking on foot, came a frightening creature known as Black Peter. He had horns on his head, a face smeared with soot, fiery red eyes, and a long red tongue. Dutch children were told that Black Peter was really the devil, whom St. Nicholas had defeated and made into his servant. On his back Black Peter carried a big sack or trunk filled with presents for children who had been good, and birch rods for those who had been bad.

Sometimes Black Peter was pictured wearing the clothes of a sixteenth-century Spanish official. This represented the unhappy period in Dutch history when the country was occupied by Spanish soldiers. The Spanish were finally driven out in the 1570s, but for

*St. Nicholas entering a Dutch town on horseback, followed by Black Peter dressed as a Spaniard. Nineteenth-century Dutch illustration by J. Schenkman.*

a long time afterward they remained a symbol of evil and oppression in Holland. By portraying Black Peter as the Spanish servant of St. Nicholas, the Dutch were reassuring themselves that Spain would never again be the master of their country.

When St. Nicholas and Black Peter arrived at a house where children lived, it was Black Peter who climbed up to the roof and dropped down through the chimney to deliver the presents and the birch rods. He put them in and around the wooden shoes that Dutch children always left by the hearth on St. Nicholas Eve. Then the sooty figure climbed back up through the chimney, and he and Nicholas went on to the next stop on their route.

The notion that Black Peter descended through chimneys to deliver his gifts probably had its roots in Dutch and German mythology. In these ancient myths, the people living in a house were blessed with good luck by ghostly creatures who could travel up and down the chimney as swiftly as smoke.

In 1624, The Dutch East India Company sent a fleet of ships to the New World and established the colony of New Netherland, with New Amsterdam—now New York City—as its capital. Along

*St. Nicholas Day morning in a Dutch home. The older brother at left is crying because he got a birch rod, while his little sister hugs her new doll. A man in the background is pointing up the chimney through which the gifts were delivered. Painting by Jan Steen.*

with their clothing and other possessions, the first Dutch settlers brought with them their most cherished traditions, including the celebration of St. Nicholas Day.

Dutch children in New Amsterdam were taught that the kindly saint would bring them presents on St. Nicholas Eve, just as he had in Holland. A Dutch ship arrived at the city's docks every year around December fifth, laden with toys, candies, and books from the mother country. Children called it the "St. Nicholas Ship" and thought the saint himself had sent it.

At St. Nicholas Eve parties in New Amsterdam, children laid out a white sheet in the parlor and waited eagerly for the arrival of a tall, thin man dressed as St. Nicholas. The children sang songs of welcome when Nicholas strode in, accompanied by a man dressed as his servant, Black Peter.

The saint scattered candies on the sheet and distributed small, wrapped presents to everyone. Meanwhile, Black Peter marched around the room, uttering low growls and shaking a bundle of birch rods. He made the children shiver when he unfolded a big burlap sack and threatened to carry off those boys and girls who had been especially bad during the year.

Before that could happen, St. Nicholas gave a command and he and Black Peter swept out the door. Then the children opened their presents, refreshments were served, and young and old alike joined in the singing and dancing.

Life in New Amsterdam changed drastically when the British, who were at war with the Dutch, seized the city in 1664 and renamed it New York. The new British residents celebrated Christmas instead of St. Nicholas Day, and told their children that Father Christmas, not St. Nicholas, brought them gifts on Christmas Eve. Descendants of the original Dutch settlers preserved many of their traditions, however, and Dutch children continued to believe in St. Nicholas—or *Sinter Claes,* as they called him for short.

As the years passed, and the British and Dutch colonists intermarried, Sinter Claes and Father Christmas gradually became blended into a single giftbringer. By the end of the Revolutionary War in 1783, he had acquired a new, American name: Santa Claus.

# CHAPTER SIX

# The Creation of
# Santa Claus

Not everyone in America knew about Santa Claus at the beginning of the 1800s. Christmas itself wasn't even celebrated in many parts of the new nation. It all depended on what country in Europe the colonists had come from, and what religious traditions they had brought with them.

Communities settled mainly by Episcopalians, Lutherans, Roman Catholics, and members of the Dutch Reformed Church usually held religious services and feasted on December twenty-fifth. Those settled by Quakers, Baptists, Congregationalists, Presbyterians, and Puritans did not. In fact, the latter groups often denounced Christmas celebrations as sinful.

The gradual acceptance of Christmas in nineteenth-century America went hand in hand with the growing popularity of Santa Claus. Four men—John Pintard, Washington Irving, Clement Clarke Moore, and Thomas Nast—were largely responsible for Santa's popularity.

The first of these men, John Pintard, was one of the founders of the New-York Historical Society. Pintard was especially interested in Dutch-American history, and on December 6, 1810, he persuaded the Society to give a festive anniversary dinner in honor of St. Nicholas. Toasts were drunk to the saint, and speakers recited the old stories about his miracles. The event proved to be such a success that it has been repeated ever since on St. Nicholas Day.

Washington Irving, the famous author of *The Legend of Sleepy Hollow,* joined the New-York Historical Society in 1808, and in 1809 he published a humorous book entitled *Diedrich Knickerbocker's History of New York from the Beginning of the World to the End of the Dutch Dynasty.* St. Nicholas is referred to a number of times in the book. According to Irving, a carving of the saint decorated the prow of the *Good Woman,* the first Dutch ship to land at New Amsterdam. Irving also said that the Dutch named the first church they built in the city the St. Nicholas Church.

SANCTE CLAUS goed heylig Man!
Trek uwe beste Tabaert aen,
Reiz daer me'e na Amsterdam,
Van Amsterdam na 'Spanje,
Daer Appelen van Oranje,
Daer Appelen van granaten,
Die rollen door de Straaten.
SANCTE CLAUS, myn goede Vriend!
Ik heb U allen tyd gedient,
Wille U my nu wat geven,
Ik zal U dienen alle myn Leven.

SAINT NICHOLAS, good holy man!
Put on the Tabard,* best you can,
Go, clad therewith, to Amsterdam,
From Amsterdam to Hispanje,
Where apples *bright* † of Oranje,
And likewise those *granate* ‡ surnam'd,
Roll through the streets, all free unclaim'd.
SAINT NICHOLAS, my dear good friend!
To serve you ever was my end,
If you will, now, me something give,
I'll serve you ever while I live.

\* Kind of jacket.　† Oranges.　‡ Pomegranates.

*Announcement of the first celebration of the Festival of St. Nicholas by the New-York Historical Society, December 6, 1810.*

In a later section of the book, Irving describes the Dutch way of celebrating St. Nicholas Day: "At this early period was instituted that pious ceremony . . . of hanging up a stocking in the chimney on St. Nicholas Eve; which stocking is always found in the morning miraculously filled—for the good St. Nicholas has ever been a great giver of gifts, particularly to children. . . ."

St. Nicholas even makes a brief appearance during a dream one of the book's characters has. The saint comes riding over the treetops in the same horse-drawn wagon he uses to bring his yearly presents to children. After landing, he lights his long Dutch pipe and reveals a future vision of New York to the startled character. Then he puts out his pipe, climbs into his wagon, flies up above the trees, and disappears.

Missing from Irving's account of St. Nicholas and his doings was any mention of Black Peter. Perhaps Irving hadn't heard about the monstrous creature, or perhaps he didn't fit in with Irving's mellow portrayal of the saint. Whatever the reason, Black Peter never became part of the St. Nicholas story in America, although he continued to play a major role in St. Nicholas Day festivities in the Netherlands.

Irving's history was read widely throughout the United States and probably did more to spread the word about St. Nicholas than any book up to that time. Some people took what Irving had written about the saint as fact. Authors of later histories stated that Nicholas's likeness had indeed appeared as the figurehead on the *Good Woman*, and that the first Dutch church in America really was named for him. In truth, these "facts" were as much a product of Washington Irving's imagination as his descriptions of the saint riding over the rooftops to deliver his gifts on St. Nicholas Eve.

Among those who read, enjoyed, and remembered Irving's portrayal of St. Nicholas was Clement Clarke Moore, author of the beloved Christmas poem, "A Visit from St. Nicholas." Who in the English-speaking world doesn't know at least the opening lines of this poem?

> *'Twas the night before Christmas,*
> *when all through the house*
> *Not a creature was stirring,*
> *not even a mouse;*
> *The stockings were hung*
> *by the chimney with care,*
> *In hopes that St. Nicholas*
> *soon would be there.*

*Engraving by T. C. Boyd from the first illustrated version of*
A VISIT FROM ST. NICHOLAS.

Clement Clarke Moore was a man of many talents. Besides writing light verse, he was an accomplished musician and professor of Greek and Hebrew literature at the General Theological Seminary in New York City. According to his granddaughter, Moore got the idea for "A Visit from St. Nicholas" while riding home one December evening in 1822 in a sleigh filled with presents for his six children.

As he listened to the sleighbells ringing on his horse's harness, Moore decided to write a poem that he could read to his family when they gathered around the fireplace on Christmas Eve. He would center it on a portrayal of St. Nicholas, inspired by the fat, jolly old Dutch handyman who used to work on the Moore family's estate.

Moore wove elements from many different sources into the poem. The idea that St. Nicholas rode in a sleigh pulled by reindeer came from an

COURTESY THE NEW-YORK HISTORICAL SOCIETY.

*Santa Claus has just one reindeer in this illustration from the 1821 book* THE CHILDREN'S FRIEND.

anonymous poem that was published in a collection, *The Children's Friend,* in 1821, a year before Moore wrote his. That poem began:

> *Old Santeclaus with much delight*
> *His reindeer drives this frosty night*
> *O'er chimney-tops and tracks of snow*
> *To bring his yearly gifts to you.*

Moore may have known the poem from reading it aloud to his own children. However, he made an important change; instead of the single reindeer who pulled Santeclaus's sleigh, Moore gave his St. Nicholas a team of "eight tiny reindeer." And eight the old saint has had ever since.

Moore had probably heard some of the old Dutch stories about St. Nicholas and Black Peter, for St. Nicholas in the poem comes down through the chimney to deliver his presents. Moore may also have read about the Swedish Christmas elf, the Jultomten, since he described St. Nicholas as looking like an elf:

> *He had a broad face and a little round belly,*
> *That shook when he laughed, like a bowlful of jelly.*
> *He was chubby and plump, a right jolly old elf,*
> *And I laughed when I saw him, in spite of myself.*

*T. C. Boyd's portrayal of Santa Claus in the first illustrated edition of A VISIT FROM ST. NICHOLAS.*

Moore took all of these elements and made an entirely new creation out of them. When he read the completed poem to his family and friends on Christmas Eve, everyone listened with close attention. One of the guests, a young woman from Troy, New York, liked it so much that she asked for a copy to take home. A year later, without identifying the author, she sent the poem to the editor of the Troy *Sentinel*. It appeared in print for the first time in the issue of December 23, 1823, accompanied by the following note: "We know not to whom we are indebted for this description of that unwearied patron of children —that homely and delightful personage of parental kindness—Santa Claus . . . but from whomsoever it may have come, we give thanks for it."

Moore was upset when the young woman sent him a copy of the newspaper and he saw his poem. He had intended it only for his own children, not a wider audience. In the next few years the poem was reprinted in many other papers, and attracted an ever-growing number of admirers who wanted to know the identity of the author. When the Troy *Sentinel* republished the poem in December 1829 as it did each Christmas, the editor announced that the author was "a gentleman and scholar of the city of New York." But he didn't name Moore.

Not until the poem appeared in 1837 in an anthology entitled "The New York Book of Poetry" was Clement C. Moore listed as its author. Later Moore himself included it in a volume of his collected poems that was published in 1844. The poem was first issued in a separate, illustrated edition in 1848. Countless other illustrated versions followed, and by 1860 "A Visit from St. Nicholas" was probably the best-known Christmas poem in the United States.

Christmas itself was much more widely celebrated by then, too. December twenty-fifth became a legal holiday in all the states and territories of the Union between 1836 and 1890. Thirteen states legalized Christmas during the troubled years of the Civil War, 1861–1865.

Charles Dickens's *A Christmas Carol* appeared in 1843 and was an instant success in America as well as England. The book's humanitarian theme appealed to readers of all faiths. Many families read the story aloud each Christmas, along with "A Visit from St. Nicholas."

The Sunday School Union, sponsored jointly by the Protestant churches, adopted Christmas as an official lesson topic in 1870. However, the Union reprimanded some children for only going to Sunday

School at Christmas when a teacher dressed as Santa Claus gave out presents. Such children were known as "Christmas bummers."

*St. Nicholas* magazine for children made its debut in November 1873, just in time for Christmas that year. The magazine was edited by Mary Mapes Dodge, author of *Hans Brinker*, and published stories by such outstanding writers as Thomas Bailey Aldrich and Louisa May Alcott.

In her editorial for the first issue, Mrs. Dodge wrote: "Hurrah for dear St. Nicholas. He has made us friends in a moment. And no wonder. Is he not the boys' and girls' own friend, the especial friend of young Americans? That he is. . . . Dear old St. Nicholas with his pet names—Santa Claus, Kriss Kringle, St. Nick, and we don't know how many others. What a host of wonderful stories are told about him . . . and what loving, cheering thoughts follow in his train."

Santa Claus acquired the nickname Kriss Kringle in a roundabout way. When immigrants from Germany and Switzerland settled in Pennsylvania in the 1700s, they brought with them the German tradition that the Christ child, or Christkindl, delivered presents to children on Christmas Eve.

As English settlers joined the Germans in their communities, the name Christkindl was gradually simplified to "Kriss Kringle." This upset many German-speaking ministers, who felt the new name insulted the Christ child. Later on, children in Pennsylvania and other places began calling St. Nicholas "Kriss Kringle," and by the 1870s it had become another name for Santa Claus.

With the mounting interest in Christmas and Santa Claus, there arose a demand for pictures of the jolly gift-bringer. One of the artists who responded to this call was the well-known political cartoonist Thomas Nast.

Born in Germany in 1844, Nast came to America with his mother and sister when he was six. The family settled down in New York City, and Nast's father joined them four years later.

Even as a boy Thomas showed a talent for drawing, and he got a job as a magazine illustrator when he was only fifteen. Before he was twenty he had earned a reputation as an outstanding cartoonist. In his cartoons, he was the first to use a donkey as the symbol of the Democratic party, and an elephant as the symbol of the Republicans.

Nast drew his first picture of Santa Claus for the Christmas issue of *Harper's Weekly* magazine in

1863. It showed a short, small Santa delivering presents to two sleeping children. Santa was dressed entirely in fur, like St. Nicholas in Moore's poem, which Nast remembered from his childhood.

From 1863 until 1886, Nast sketched a new picture of Santa Claus each year for *Harper's Weekly*. In 1864, during the Civil War, Santa wore a star-covered jacket and striped trousers as he handed out Christmas gifts to Union soldiers.

Nast was the first person to draw Santa's workshop and show him keeping records of good and bad children, and answering the stack of letters that children wrote to him. In his Christmas illustration for 1882, Nast was also the first to say that Santa lived at the North Pole. The Pole was much in the news at the time, with British, Russian, and Scandinavian explorers all competing to be the first to reach it.

Because of his German background, Nast occasionally drew the Christkindl, whom he called the "Christkindchen." But his most popular pictures were the ones he made of Santa Claus. As the years passed, Santa's appearance gradually changed. From the elf-like creature of Clement Moore's poem, he was transformed by Nast's pen into the jolly, bearded man we're familiar with today.

Santa Claus delivering presents to two sleeping children. Drawing by Thomas Nast, 1863.

Santa Claus visits a Union Army camp. Drawing by Thomas Nast, 1864.

*Santa Claus reading letters from children. Drawing by Thomas Nast.*

In 1890, Nast's holiday pictures for *Harper's Weekly* were gathered together and published in a book entitled *Christmas Drawings for the Human Race*. The book proved to be extremely popular and helped to establish Nast's image of Santa Claus in the minds of adults and children all across the country. From then on few Americans would think of St. Nicholas as the tall, thin Bishop of Myra. Instead he would always be Thomas Nast's Santa Claus with his red fur-trimmed jacket, full white beard, and twinkling smile.

# CHAPTER SEVEN

# Santa Claus Everywhere

**B**y the end of the nineteenth century, Santa Claus had become as familiar a symbol in America as Uncle Sam.

On Christmas Eve or Christmas morning, many fathers dressed up as Santa Claus, filled a sack with presents, and marched into the living room with a cheery "Ho! Ho! Ho!" Even President Benjamin Harrison played Santa Claus. In 1891 he told a White House correspondent: "We shall have an old-fashioned Christmas tree for the grandchildren upstairs, and I shall be their Santa Claus myself. If my influence goes for aught, let me hope that my example may be followed in every family in the land."

Whether at the White House or in a modest home a thousand miles away, children delighted in seeing Santa Claus in person. But inevitably there came a Christmas—earlier for some children, later for others—when they ceased to believe in Santa Claus.

This loss of faith confused and upset many children. In 1897 it led one little girl, Virginia O'Hanlon of New York City, to write a letter to the editor of the *New York Sun*. Her letter, which soon became famous, read:

*Dear Editor:*

*I am eight years old. Some of my little friends say there is no Santa Claus. Papa says, "If you see it in the* Sun *it's so." Please tell me the truth, is there a Santa Claus?*

The *Sun* answered her letter with an editorial by Francis P. Church that became equally famous, and was reprinted in the *Sun* every Christmas until the newspaper ceased publication in 1950.

"Yes, Virginia, there is a Santa Claus," Church wrote. "He exists as certainly as love and generosity and devotion exist, and you know that they abound and give to your life its highest beauty and joy. Alas!

How dreary would be the world if there were no Santa Claus. It would be as dreary as if there were no Virginias."

Church went on to say: "The most real things in the world are those that neither children nor men can see. Did you ever see fairies dancing on the lawn? Of course not, but that's no proof that they are not there. Nobody can conceive or imagine all the wonders that are unseen and unseeable in the world."

He concluded: "Thank God he [Santa Claus] lives, and he lives forever. A thousand years from now, Virginia, nay, ten times 10,000 years from now, he will continue to make glad the heart of childhood."

As America entered the twentieth century, the image of Santa Claus was everywhere. It appeared on Christmas cards, in cartoons and magazine illustrations, and on stereopticon slides that produced a three-dimensional effect. Santa was shown making toys in his North Pole workshop and going over lists of good and bad children. Other photos showed him arriving in town in one of the newfangled automobiles instead of a sleigh. There was even a picture of him riding on a sled pulled by two turkeys!

In the early 1900s, people began to focus on

*THIS PAGE AND OPPOSITE: Stereopticon slides showing Santa Claus in his workshop and going over lists of good children.*

*Santa Claus arriving in Independence, Iowa, in a car.*

*Santa in Michigan, riding on a sled pulled by two turkeys.*

the needs of children, and laws were passed that restricted or prohibited child labor. Along with these developments, the notion arose that every child had the right to a joyful Christmas. Santa Claus quickly became the chief symbol of this trend. Men dressed as Santa stood on busy street corners, ringing bells and collecting money for organizations like the Salvation Army that gave presents to poor families. Other Santas were hired by department stores to greet long lines of children, dandle them on their knees, and ask them what they wanted for Christmas.

*A Salvation Army Santa on a New York City street, 1915.*
THE LIBRARY OF CONGRESS.

*Santa Claus talking with children in Macy's department store, New York, 1942. Photo by Marjory Collins.*

To meet the demand for Santa Clauses, special training schools were set up around the country. They taught people how to play Santa Claus in department stores, at hospital parties, and on other public occasions.

In 1956, a national retail organization, Sales Promotions, Inc., issued a list of guidelines for department store Santa Clauses:

1. Santa must never kiss a child.
2. Santa's hands and fingernails must be immaculately clean at all times.
3. Santa must never bribe a child to be good by promising toys.
4. Santa must never threaten a child.
5. Santa must make no promises unless he knows they can be fulfilled.
6. Santa must not frighten timid children with roaring laughter.
7. Santa should have tissue handkerchiefs available for children with sniffles.

If children couldn't see Santa Claus in person to tell him what they wanted for Christmas, many wrote him letters addressed to the North Pole. Parents often intercepted these letters, read them, and did their best to satisfy their child's desires. But thousands of letters got into the mail, where they ended up in the dead letter office of the Post Office.

Not wanting the children who wrote the letters to be disappointed, various individuals and groups volunteered to answer them. One such group was the Santa Claus Association, whose chief goal was "to preserve children's faith in Santa Claus."

Founded in New York City in 1914, the Association obtained letters addressed to Santa Claus from the Post Office and sought information about the children who had written them. If the field workers reported that a child wasn't likely to receive any presents, the Association tried to provide some from its warehouse. People from all over New York contributed money to the Association to help pay for the presents.

In 1928, the federal postal authorities investigated the Association and criticized its business practices. After that the New York City Post Office refused to turn over any more letters to the Association, but postal employees organized their own letter-answering campaign in its place. Other groups and localities also continued to answer children's letters to Santa Claus. One of the best-known of these was the small village of Santa Claus, Indiana.

Named Santa Claus in 1927, and given national publicity in a "Ripley's Believe It or Not" cartoon in 1929, the village is the home of fewer than a hundred people. However, more than 300,000 tourists each

*Santa Claus with reindeer in the theme park at Santa Claus, Indiana.*

year visit its theme park, Santa Claus Land, which features Santa's workshop on Kriss Kringle Street and the world's largest statue of Santa Claus. The statue stands twenty-three feet tall, weighs forty-two tons, and has the following inscription at its base:

DEDICATED

TO THE CHILDREN OF THE WORLD

IN

MEMORY OF AN UNDYING LOVE

Every December the Santa Claus post office receives more than five million pieces of Christmas mail. Most of these are personal and corporate Christmas cards, which are trucked to Santa Claus, canceled with the village's postmark, and then sent to their destinations.

The rest of the mail consists of letters from children who have heard of the village and think that Santa must live there. When the letters started coming, back in the 1930s, the postmaster himself tried to answer them. As the number increased, local people offered to help him. Each year more and more letters flooded into the post office, though. At last the postmaster, a member of the American Legion, turned to Legion posts in neighboring communities for help.

Today Legion volunteers throughout Indiana read and answer the more than 100,000 letters that children send to Santa Claus every December. All of their replies are returned to the village for mailing so that the envelopes will bear the famous Santa Claus postmark.

As the years passed, new characters became part of the Santa Claus legend. In many Christmas stories and illustrations, a flock of elves surrounded Santa in his workshop and helped him make toys for the world's children. Later Santa Claus acquired a wife, Mrs. Claus, who was as fat and jolly as her husband. But probably the most famous twentieth-century addition to Santa's family was Rudolph, the Red-Nosed Reindeer, who made his debut at Christmastime in 1939.

Rudolph was the creation of Robert L. May, an advertising copywriter for Montgomery Ward & Company. The company wanted something new and different for Santa Claus to hand out to the thousands of children who visited him in the Ward stores. May came up with a story in verse about Rudolph, the reindeer with the shiny-red nose. Santa's other reindeer made fun of Rudolph until one foggy Christmas Eve when Santa, seeing Rudolph's nose aglow, asked him to lead the rest of the herd across the dark night sky.

The story was illustrated with whimsical drawings and printed in booklet form in the fall of 1939.
That Christmas over 2,400,000 copies were given

*Rudolph, the Red-Nosed Reindeer as he was pictured in the original
Montgomery Ward & Co. booklet, 1939.*

away free to children, who responded at once to the story's ugly duckling theme. Ward distributed 3,600,000 more copies when it reprinted the booklet for Christmas, 1946.

Robert May obtained the copyright to Rudolph's story in 1947, and it appeared as a hardcover book a few months later. Then, in 1949, Gene Autry recorded a song about Rudolph that climbed to the top of the Hit Parade. Other singers performed "Rudolph," and within a few years over 50,000,000 records of the song had been sold.

Rudolph's fame increased even more after an animated film of his adventures was televised in 1964. The movie is shown again almost every Christmas, and has helped to make Rudolph a familiar character to children all over the world.

Santa Claus himself is still the best-known and most popular of all the characters who have come to be associated with Christmas. Not everyone is in favor of him, though.

Some psychologists, for example, claim that Santa Claus does harm to children because he makes them think good things will come to them without their having to work for them. Other psychologists, however, say that a belief in Santa expands the imaginations of children.

Probably the strongest opponents of Santa Claus are those who feel that, over the years, he has become more a symbol of commercialism than of unselfish gift giving. These people charge that the widespread use of Santa's image in newspapers, magazines, and on television is mainly a gimmick to help sell Christmas merchandise.

In 1984, there was even an attempt to use the image of Santa Claus in a horror movie. The film, *Silent Night, Deadly Night*, told the story of a crazed killer who wore a Santa suit when he committed his crimes. Angry parents all over the U.S. picketed theaters where the movie was playing. They argued that it would have a bad effect on children, making them think of Santa Claus not as a kindly old man but as someone to fear. Their protests, along with poor business at the box office, forced the distributor to withdraw the film from circulation.

Despite such assaults on Santa's good name and reputation, he continues to reappear in many different forms each December. Homeless men from the shelters maintained by the Volunteers of America dress up in red suits and collect money for charity on the

WAGNER–INTERNATIONAL PHOTOS COURTESY OF VOLUNTEERS OF AMERICA

*Volunteers of America Santa Clauses marching to their posts.*

streets of New York and other cities. Many unemployed actors, singers, and dancers portray Santa in New York, Chicago, and Los Angeles department stores. Retired persons enjoy impersonating him in the stores and shopping malls of the South and Southwest. People who speak Spanish and other languages are hired to play Santa in places that have large bilingual populations.

Santa Claus's popularity extends far beyond the borders of the United States. When American soldiers went abroad to fight during the First and Second World Wars, they carried the idea of Santa with them. Movies and television have spread his fame even farther. Today red-suited Santas take part in holiday celebrations from Sydney, Australia, to Stockholm, Sweden; from Anchorage, Alaska, to Buenos Aires, Argentina. He is even known in Turkey, where his ancestor, Nicholas, lived so long ago.

A Santa-like figure, Grandfather Frost, brings presents to children in the Soviet Union, too. Grandfather Frost has no religious meaning, and comes on New Year's Eve rather than Christmas Eve. But like Santa he is usually portrayed as a chubby man with a white beard, dressed in red, fur-trimmed clothes.

Over the centuries, Santa Claus's appearance and personality have changed to suit the changing needs of the people who believed in him. From the kindly Bishop of Myra who could perform miracles, he became the tall, stern St. Nicholas who rewarded good children and punished those who had been bad. Later, in America, he was transformed into the jolly gift-bringer who had presents for everyone, whether they'd been good or not. Now, on some greeting cards, he is pictured doing up-to-date things like biking, jogging, and checking children's names on his computer.

Chances are Santa Claus will continue to change in future years, as people themselves change. But whether he gets thinner or fatter, or travels by rocket instead of reindeer, no doubt he'll remain the world's most beloved symbol of Christmas cheer and generosity.

# *Bibliography*

Ancelet-Hustache, Jeanne. *Saint Nicholas.* Translated by Rosemary Sheed. New York: The Macmillan Company, 1962.

Auld, William Muir. *Christmas Traditions.* New York: The Macmillan Company, 1931.

Barnett, James H. *The American Christmas.* New York: The Macmillan Company, 1954.

Coffin, Tristram Potter. *The Book of Christmas Folklore.* New York: The Seabury Press, 1973.

Del Re, Gerard and Patricia. *The Christmas Almanack.* New York: Doubleday & Company, Inc., 1979.

Ebon, Martin. *St. Nicholas, Life and Legend.* New York: Harper & Row, Publishers, Inc., 1975.

Hosking, Arthur N. *The Night Before Christmas: The True Story of "A Visit from St. Nicholas" with a Life of the Author, Clement C. Moore.* New York: Dodd, Mead & Company, 1934.

Jones, Charles W. *Saint Nicholas of Myra, Bari, and Manhattan: Biography of a Legend.* Chicago: The University of Chicago Press, 1978.

Krythe, Maymie R. *All About Christmas.* New York: Harper & Brothers, 1954.

Moore, Anne Carroll. *Nicholas: A Manhattan Christmas Story.* New York: G. P. Putnam's Sons, 1924.

Muir, Frank. *Christmas Customs and Traditions.* New York: Taplinger Publishing Company, 1977.

Myers, Robert J. *Celebrations: The Complete Book of American Holidays.* New York: Doubleday & Company, Inc., 1972.

*Thomas Nast's Christmas Drawings.* Introduction by Thomas Nast St. Hill. New York: Dover Publications, Inc., 1978.

Nettel, Reginald. *Santa Claus.* London: Gordon Fraser, 1957.

Pauli, Hertha. *St. Nicholas' Travels.* Illustrated by Susanne Suba. Boston: Houghton Mifflin Company, 1945.

Scullard, H. H. *Festivals and Ceremonies of the Roman Republic.* Ithaca, N.Y.: Cornell University Press, 1981.

Van Nierop, Henriette. *Santa Claus the Dutch Way.* New York: Netherlands Information Service, 1955.

Weiser, Francis X. *The Christmas Book.* New York: Harcourt, Brace & World, Inc., 1952.

Wernecke, Herbert H. *Christmas Customs Around the World.* Philadelphia: The Westminster Press, 1954, 1975.

# *Index*

Page numbers in *italics* refer to illustrations.